NO MORE TOMORROW

The word your heart craves,
but your soul denies

Anshuman Vashist

Cover Design: Neha Bhati

INDIA • SINGAPORE • MALAYSIA

ISBN
Paperback 979-8-89632-839-1
Hardcase 979-8-89699-759-7

For my mummy I love you I am always
blessed with your blessing I am always
at the heavens of your
feet
You are my everything my universe

For You if you are reading this
I love you to infinity and beyond

I held them high, like a monarch on their
throne,
Gave them my world, so they'd never feel
alone.
Love, respect, devotion—all that I knew,
Wrapped in my warmth, like a gentle dew.

Yet in the end, they painted me dark,
The villain they'd mark, with a merciless spark.
Stripped of my heart, left hollow and cold,
In suffering's grip, with stories untold.

Now I walk wounded, a soul turned to stone,
A heart once of gold, now aching alone.

My heart's flower hadn't fully
blossomed, yet you stopped
nourishing it.
What kind of person does
that—breaks a heart and then
gives up on love entirely.

My gaze also turns toward
those places; what can I do?
Your beauty is still captivating,
but what can I do?

Since you left, I can't find sleep,
My heart feels restless in the
quiet night.
Were you the only one for me,
Whose absence hurts me deep
inside?

Now, where can I find
someone like you, To love me
with that same bright spark?
You've given me hope for a
new love, But can I trust this
feeling in my heart?
Your promise speaks of a love
so true, But I still feel alone
and lost.
How can I believe when I can't
find peace, That anyone could
love me like you did?

Your memories crash over me
once more—
tell me, what am I supposed to
do?
My heart aches to see you
again, but how can I carry it
to you? I know you'll never
be mine, yet how am I meant
to live without you?

I'm lost in the search for you,
unsure where to stop.
Then I see a figure standing
alone, I ask him about you,
And he replies, "I don't know
the one you seek,
But when you feel love, that's
where you should rest."

I, too, sent love's messenger to
their door,
To see if they were happier
than before.
But even love's angel returned
broken and torn,
Saying, "They're happier now
than when you were born.

While you ache as if life's gone
astray,
They thrive as though you
were never in their way.

You're lucky to have the moon,
but me?
I hold the universe in my
hands— because I have you

Wish me luck to find
forgiveness, for what you did
to my heart.
Shattered it into a thousand
pieces— yet each piece, still
aching, loves you anew.
A thousand times over, in a
thousand broken ways

The world begins to look brighter, warmer, When you start becoming better, For you are the world you live within; Others are but passing moments— Fleeting days that shape it, Either painting it beautiful, or casting it in shadows.

You left me as if I never
mattered, You said,
“Forget me and move on.”
But how can I let go of a love
I wanted to cherish for a
lifetime?
How can you expect me to
forget the moon and simply
live among the stars?

Just once more, let me feel
your embrace—
come close, hold me in this
trembling space.
I'm waiting here, hoping you'll
return, even if it's just to break
my heart again,
come back once more… and
let me burn.

Though it's not what others
may deem right,
Deep down, I find myself in
this plight.

I crave no diamonds, I seek no
gold, Just your love, a treasure
more precious than told.
For all I desire, through the
highs and lows, Is your heart's
warmth, where true love flows.

In a world of riches, it's clear
to see,
All I truly want is your love,
only from thee.

If I could reach the sky, I'd lay
it at your feet.
If I ever found love, I'd give
you every piece of it.
I'd hand you the seven
wonders, and offer you
everything I have.

I'd take all your pain and suffer
in silence, just to give you my
life, every breath of it.
But even then, I know it
wouldn't be enough to make
you stay.

I thought you were the long
journey that would turn my
life into a beautiful pilgrimage.
But you walked just a few
miles with me, then let go of
my hand, as if I needed to find
a way to move on without you.
It feels like I took a ride to a
place far away, leaving behind
everything we shared.

I am the water they need to
survive,
A quiet stream, to keep them
alive.
But they crave the wine, rich
and rare,
Chasing its thrill, unaware of
the snare.

They sip indulgence, fleeting
and fine,
While I, the water, wait by the
line.
For when the wine fades, and
thirst draws near,
They'll find only emptiness,
not solace here.

I've tasted love in every shade
and hue,
But don't teach me to love
anew.
I've lived through dying,
crawled through despair,
Revived myself, but don't bury
me there.

I see myself shattered in the
mirror's stare,
Haunted by pieces too broken
to bear.
How can I look at the face that
caused this ache,
The one who left my soul to
break?

Perhaps a trace of betrayal
lingers in me,
For you walked away, yet still,
you breathe in me.

They said I don't have a future, that I'm just wasting my time, Chilling, doing nothing to secure what we could be. And then they walked away, leaving me in silence. I know they're right; their words echo in my mind. But what about me?

All those promises of endless night walks, Eating ice cream while watching TV— They forgot them all, all because they lost faith in me. I wish they could see the longing in my eyes Every time I looked at them, dreaming of a future together, Imagining all the little things that would make them happy.

But now, those dreams feel like shadows, haunting me in their absence, a bittersweet reminder -Of what we could have built—if only they had believed.

What should I wish for in a
world where you don't exist?
What use is a God who cannot
bring you to me?
What meaning do words hold
if they don't carry your name?
How can I write any verse
where your presence isn't felt?

Today, in my prayers, I asked
for their company once again,
Asked for a chance to meet
them as a stranger, unknown,
To love them anew, filling my
heart with what was lost,
And to bring one last chance
for me to become the person
They always wished for, the
one they deserved.

I prayed for a moment,
Where they wouldn't
remember my name,
So I could love them without
the weight of our past,
To fall for them again, and to
feel that spark last,
If only to become, for a fleeting
time,
The soul they always dreamed
of—their perfect rhyme.

I asked them, “What would happen if I were to face life without you?” They looked at me and said, “Then die.” And in that moment, I did. What do you mean I’m still alive? This body breathes, but the one who loved them— with every shattered piece— is long gone.

I hope we don't meet again,
for I don't know who I'll be
this time—
the one who loved you
endlessly or the one you left
wounded.
I'm afraid of meeting both.

Love isn't a choice—it's a feeling, Built on trust, care, and unspoken dreams. If someone claims you didn't love them enough, It isn't your fault, nor a failure to be.

They wanted you to be divine, flawless, While they loved you with a darkness, raw and wild. Expecting light when giving shadows— A love that's never tender, but fierce and defiled.

Break me as much as you
will— still, my heart chooses
you.
Not out of foolishness, but
because I once begged God for
you.
And now, I cannot bring
myself to beg to forget.

Why should I bow only to
you—are you the only god I
have?
Why should I love only you—
are you the only life I have?

It's almost tragic, isn't it? That
you find joy in watching me
hurt,
and I find mine in seeing
you happy, even if it's from
breaking me

To trust you was a sin, it
seems,
The pain you gave shattered
my dreams.

You broke my heart, then
claimed regret,
A fragile soul—its end was
met.

They read my verses,
and mistake you for my God,
calling me a fool in love,
a soul is undone, a heart too
flawed.

They say the faith I gave you,
as if you were divine,
only showed how small I was—
a shadow in your shrine.

How can I tell this world of
ours
what you were meant to be?
A flame, a storm, a fleeting
star—
you were all of that to me.

Perhaps it's mercy that you left,
to humble what was proud.
Now this head bows to God
alone,
no longer to the crowd.

Should I ever bow to mortal
hands,
to love untrue, misplaced—
know then, that I have given
all,
and vanished without a trace.

Face-to-face stood that soul,
Screaming, desperate to escape
the pain.
I splashed water on my face,
Struggling to wake myself
again.

Drowning deeper in the ache,
While in the mirror,
They stood, staring back at
me—
A smile laced with bitter grief.

They whispered, "This pain is
sweet,
It comes from love,
incomplete."
With tears glistening in their
eyes,
They pointed at me, accusing,
A silent cry.

Lost in the thoughts of love,
pain, betrayal,
I let a fragile smile linger.
And the soul before me,
Kept screaming, their agony a
haunting trigger.

A thousand times I tell
myself—
you are no longer mine.
Yet a part of my heart still lives
in you,
hidden, stubborn, intertwined.

When sorrow shadows your
face,
my soul trembles, afraid.
But when you smile at another,
it feels as if the heavens have
betrayed.

Your joy, your pain— still rule
my skies.
No matter how far I run,
your shadow never dies.

Love stood waiting at the door,
longing to step inside.
Death lingered by my bedside,
eager to steal my breath.

I called out into the silence,
but you chose to walk away.
Seeing my heart steeped in
sorrow,
love turned back from the
threshold,
and even death refused to
meet my gaze.

One last request I make to you,
For every beat, my heart holds true.
In love's embrace, I breathe, I live,
Yet without you, I break, I give.

I've loved you more than words convey,
More than life itself, more each day.
Please, I beg, don't let me fall—
Don't paint me dark before them all.

In this world, don't make me vile,
Don't cast me in a villain's trial.
For love's pure fire has been my own,
And no heart but yours have I ever known.

So I plead, in love's defense,
Don't make me live in deep offense.
Don't turn me into what I fear—
A villain lost, insincere.

You're loving me with all you
have, while I drift further away
from you.
Could it be that I am God,
the one you worship, yet one
who feels nothing at all?

Don't look at me with those beautiful eyes,
Don't lift me in your arms to the skies.
For then, I can no longer wait,
For anyone else or a different fate.

Why did you hold me close and take me high,
Why whisper words of love I can't deny?
They echo still, in every thought,
A melody I wish I had forgotten.

I once believed love was never deserved,
No soul on Earth could truly serve.
But then, like a god, you took my hand,
And I drowned in words I couldn't withstand.

Through streets and temples, I wandered wide,
Searching for you, with no one to guide.
But all I found was pain, unspoken,
And the shards of a heart, forever broken.

The one who once sang my
sorrows away,
is no longer the one who walks
my way.

In the quiet of nights, I write
of them still,
the one who no longer lights
my days with their will.

They could never trust the love
I gave,
though I believed, my all, I'd
save.
But how could they trust when
I myself knew—
I was never truly mine to
pursue.

These eyes of yours, like cascading
streams,
For whom do they brim with
silent dreams?
Is it a spectacle of someone's end,
Or the farewell of a love that won't
mend?

Which flame was lit, only to fade
away,
Or whose call beckoned, then led
astray?
Why did you turn back while
walking with me,
Leaving me lost in this endless plea?

What chaos brews, what war
ignites,
What secret pain does the silence
fight?
Tonight, I've invited death to dine,
For my love bears the scars of time.

The one I adored through years
and tears,
Now weds another, fulfilling fears.
Is this my demise for the
world to see,
Or my love's final farewell
to me?

Thank you so much for being
there for me.
Thank you for giving me
memories I once only dreamed
of.
I know we're not meant to be
together,
But those memories are what
make me feel alive again.

I'm grateful for everything you
did for me.
And I'm sorry—for just being
myself. I know you didn't like
that side of me, yet still, thank
you for enduring it all with me.

Always yours.

Even now, in the hollow ache
you left behind, I clutch the
ghost of dreams that fade with
each break of dawn. I stand
on the fragile edge of night,
whispering to the darkness,
hoping the universe might
shatter, might somehow
realign, just to bring you back.

I wait, foolish and fractured,
casting silent pleas into the
vast, indifferent stars, lost in
the echo of all that's gone. Here
I remain—a shadow bound to
a memory—still yours, even as
I fade in the absence of you.

Those who've tasted love's
bitter betrayal,
Know the flavor of poison
well—
A slow burn, a silent scream,
A wound where shadows
dwell.

But those untouched by love's
cruel sting,
In death find gentle rest—
A quiet peace, a soft release,
As if by sorrow blessed.

I did everything we once did
together,
Not in dreams, but in a world
unshaken by forever.

Your leaving didn't change who
I became,
In love, I remained, honoring
your name.
Even after you left, my heart
stayed true,
Loving the memories, as if they
were you.

The village whispers Love is
the deadliest disease,
Yet I wander their street daily,
as if with ease.
I steal glances, only to turn
away,
What a vagabond I am,
flaunting my decay.

Today, their lane is adorned,
aglow with light,
Perhaps I've come for one final
sight.
They depart, their absence
heavy in my chest,
Yet I'll return, drawn by their
lingering scent, and unrest.

This morning, I woke from a
world of despair,
Where even in dreams, they
were never there.
Lost to another, their laughter
so bright,
While I stood alone in the
shadows of night.

What curse is this, that I
cannot find rest?
Their absence carved hollows
deep in my chest.
In waking, they haunt; in sleep,
they betray,
Leaving me empty, night after
day.

A plea of love has been placed,
Let my counsel too be
embraced.
Let God deliver the final
decree,
And poets gather in their
symphony.

The heavens have sent an
advocate for me,
From the ministry bearing my
name's plea.
I've been sentenced to death,
they proclaim,
For my love has been nailed, a
martyr in shame.

Yet, as the judge spoke my fate
aloud,
Even he faltered, his head
unbowed.
"You may die," he said, his
voice a plea,
"But no grave will set you free
From the chains of memories'
eternity"

Your thought becomes an
endless tide,
Yet in words, it chooses to
hide.

I try to weave you into lines,
But silence drowns these
fragile rhymes.

Your scent, your voice—my
only world,
Beyond this, no thought can be
unfurled.

If you'd embrace me, whisper
my name,
I'd write a saga, a timeless
flame.
But without you, the page stays
bare,
Not a single word would dare
appear.

The confession of love has
taken place,
May God show mercy, grant
His grace. For it's you—only
you—I've come to embrace.

After you, I search for
someone like you,
Who could give me pain, yet it
wouldn't feel like pain?
Someone who could weave
dreams in my weary eyes,
And ask for nothing, but
everything, again.

After you, I search for
someone like you,
Who could love without
demanding love in return?
Someone who, with just their
presence,
Could make my broken world
unbroken, unburned.

After you, I search for
someone like you,
Who'd call me theirs and truly
be mine?
Someone who, in the ruins of
my soul,
Could teach me to breathe, to
heal, to shine.

These tears betray me,
yet I let them fall—silent, free.
They speak of ruin, a story
unkind,
but also the strength I now find.

Someone may rejoice in my
despair,
but I rise, unbroken, from their
snare.
Love and passion, mere fleeting
lies,
I've cast them away, let illusions
die.

Go ahead, reveal your deceit,
I've crushed my heart beneath my
feet.
Your picture, now ashes in the
flame,
marks the end of your hollow
claim.

The ocean of pain begins to
recede,
your promises, mere echoes I no
longer need.
You may have claimed a victory
steeped in spite,
but in my ruin, I've found my light.

Pain evades me, yet it haunts
my soul,
Nights pass by, but sleep takes
no control.
The sorrow they left, I cannot
understand,
Yet I still pray for them with
trembling hands.

Wrapped in white, yet peace
won't stay,
Perhaps love's torment has
drifted away.

This place is still as beautiful,
come and see someday,
My love for you remains just
as deep—if you ever find your
way.

You had said that you are not
like others,
You knew that I always found
pain in love.
You always said that you will
be mine forever,
But you went away and left me
in the deepest pain.

You knew that this world never
gave me love,
Yet you made me yours by
giving me love,
And when I became only
yours,
You left me alone.

Shameless, I stand, drenched in despair,
Your scorn like thorns, yet I remain there.
Love spills from my soul, wild and unchained,
While your words, "I hate you," leave me drained.

What is this hatred, sharp and cruel,
That keeps your shadow my constant duel?
I held a falling star, its glow in my hand,
A fragile gift—a silent demand.

You once whispered, "When a star breaks free,
Close your eyes and wish for me."
But the wish to bind you, to make you stay,
Shattered like that star and slipped away.

Now the heavens mourn, and so do I,
A love unspoken, left to die.

After you, I never loved
anyone the way I loved, Never
gave another the worth they
once had. Holding you above
all—was it a punishment I
carved for myself? For I never
let anyone else become even a
shadow of what you were.

The air is thick with whispers,
wild and sweet,
Of drunken haze, desires
incomplete.
A season of madness, longing's
flame,
And your silent departure—a
lover's blame.

I've seen the reckless, the lost,
the stray,
Every shade of mischief comes
my way.
But nothing broke me quite
the same,
As watching you fade, claiming
another's name.

Draped in red, adorned for
another,
A veil hiding vows meant to
smother.
For one glimpse of you
beneath that guise,
I even abandoned my prayers
to the skies.

I never lost, not even where all
others fell,
I didn't bow, not even where
faith itself knelt as well.
I carried the pride of being
unbeaten, the world spun in
awe,
But I was defeated where love
rose with its unyielding law

I once believed that without
you, everything would fall
apart,
And when you left, that fear
became my reality.
Losing you was my greatest
nightmare,
Now that you're gone, I
wonder—what power could
keep me alive?

If I had passed time like he did,
I'd be happy today,
I wouldn't be living like this—
dying a little more each day.

Don't lose yourself completely,
You're still so precious, don't
cry so much.

Today was just a bad day for
love,
The day is gone, my friend—
Don't be so heartbroken.

Today, I let your memories
drench me in the rain once
more,
But this time, the rain fell from
my eyes.

I stood beneath the storm,
hoping to wash you away,
Yet every drop whispered your
name.
The sky cried for me, because I
couldn't cry enough, And even
the clouds knew—
I'm still drowning in you.

Why can't I find peace?
Was that the only soul meant for me,
wandering this wide world?
Is that why my heart aches,
restless in the silence?
I search for comfort in every corner, yet nothing feels like home.
Were they the only light in this endless night?
Because now, everything is hollow, emptied of warmth.
How does life go on when the one who meant everything is gone?
Or is it that I've forgotten
how to live in a world without them?

you can choose a new
companion for your journey,
But my love was true, a bond I
couldn't sever.
Though time moves on, and
paths may diverge,
I was never given permission
to love again,
To heal or to dream, to find
another.

A friend asked, “Did it hurt when they broke your heart?”

I smiled and replied, “In that moment of parting, The light in their eyes was so achingly bright, That I forgot my own heart was hurting.

In this world, the passion to
live felt hollow and bare,
Without you, each moment
turned to sorrow's snare.
I wished to write love as a
beautiful tale,
But after you left, love felt like
a sin I couldn't unveil.

On one side, the moon and
stars,
On the other, the sun's harsh
light,
But your eyes, with their glow,
Outshine the whole world's
sight.

On one side, the price of
pearls,
On the other, a necklace of
gold,
Yet none of it compares,
To the smile your lips hold.

There's no tomorrow, just the
quiet of the night,
Where dreams once bloomed,
now lost in endless flight.
The sun won't rise to mend the
fractured sky,
And the promises we made
will fade and die.

No more second chances, no
paths left to choose,
No more hearts to heal,
nothing left to lose.
The stars might still shine, but
they won't lead me back,
In this darkness, I walk a
lonely track.

Yesterday lingers like a ghost I
can't reach,
Today slips away, like sand off
a beach.
There's no tomorrow, no hope
to borrow,
Just silence, and a heart heavy
with sorrow.

You've moved on, but is joy
what you've found?
You tell me not to speak—
what's buried deep, unbound?
Go on, move forward, but
should I still seek
A truth that's veiled in silence,
bitter, bleak?
Your memories linger, heavy in
my chest,
Yet if you're content, what
more could I request?
I watch you leave, but my heart
still fights,
Chasing shadows of you
through endless nights.

Someone teach me how to love
again,
Someone make me whole
again, just for them.

Make it so they can't live
without me,
Someone show me that magic
spell,
Where I can write their
name, And they'll follow me
wherever I dwell.
And when I bow my head in
prayer,
Let someone lift it, and bring
them there.

Oh God, let me drift into
quiet, a soft release from this
ache—
I don't want to see them again,
don't want to feel this hollow
pulse of life's cruel rhythm.
I am tired, craving only peace,
a stillness to hold me safe from
the hurt.
Yet, my heart whispers,

"Be silent, let me ache
again. If they return to tear
me open, isn't it a strange,
sweet pleasure to burn in
their hands?"

You were my faith in love, But since you, I've lost my will to live. Love is everything to me, Yet for you, it's just another chance, While for me, it's the final heartbreak, A sorrow I can no longer forgive.

I've been filled with hurt since you left me, The rain still falls, beautiful and pure, But I've lost its beauty, lost the scent Of the wet earth's tender allure. The rainbow, once a lover's vow, Now fades to colors dull and gray, No longer does its arc ignite The dreams we shared, swept away.

It's not the pain that dulls my gaze, But the love and joy that's gone astray— Ever since I lost you, life lost its hue, And color slipped into endless gray.

The world is brimming with joy, yet all I need is found in you— in the light of your eyes as I lose myself, watching you endlessly, in the breath of air touched by your presence, lingering like a quiet ache. For me, joy and happiness are one and the same, and they will always be… only you.

I've turned from the moon,
now I speak to the stars,
You may no longer pray for
me, wherever you are.
But I call your name in every
breath I take,
While you forget me with ease,
like a passing mistake.
I too wish to erase you, as
you've erased me,
Yet even in trying, your
memory sets me free.

You chose another's warmth,
another's laughter, and here I
am—
still rooted in place, watching
the empty sky.
I wait for a single, trembling
star to fall, hoping to catch its
fleeting light, just to wish for
you.

If I ever meet God, I'll surely
ask— why does too much love
change a person?
Doesn't the bond mean
anything, or is love only what
we can show, not what we feel
in our hearts?
What is this "too much
love"? Someone, please tell
me, so that maybe one day,
someone will love me that way,
the way it changed them.

If I had known it was the last
time,
I would have held you,
endlessly,
Until infinity lost its meaning,
And time slipped away in
silence.

Why does every night bring
you back to me,
Haunting me with memories
that refuse to set me free?
Tell the moon to stay by your
side,
Let me burn under the sun,
while you bask in its light.
Stop visiting me in these
endless dreams,
For fear that one day, while
watching you there,
I might lose myself completely,
fading away into despair.

I don't know why the sun
doesn't burn me anymore.
Maybe it knows I'm already
scorched by the pain you left
behind. I'm hurt so deeply now
that even the sun's heat feels
like a gentle, cooling breeze,
as if it's trying to soothe me—
trying to give me a moment's
calm, a brief escape from the
fire you set within me.

If you call, and I don't come,
Could that ever truly be?
If you ask me to stay, and I
walk away,
Could that really be me?

If you say, 'Love me,' and I turn
away,
Such a day will never arise.
And if you say, 'Leave,' I'll only
reply,
'Not now, not ever, not in this
life.

They used to tell me that my
eyes were deep, that they could
see everything in them.
But when they left me alone at
the metro station, I don't know
what they saw in them then.

Maybe they forgot to look
for the pain, raw and red like
blood, pleading with them to
stay, just once more, to say
they loved me.
But they turned away, leaving
me there with nothing but the
hollow echo of their absence

The angel of love, wandering
in the heavens, still believes
they've gifted humanity its
rarest treasure.

If only someone could tell
them—down here, their
precious love has been sold to
the marketplace, stripped of its
soul, traded like any common
thing."

Tell me the weight of my
broken heart,
Show me how to live, tearing
myself apart.
I wish I could love someone
else as much as I loved you—
Make someone as dear to me
as you used to be, if you can,
too.

Please show me your
spellbound eyes,
Let me have a glimpse, of your
face I idolize.
These eyes ache for the sight of
you—
If I can't have you, life will bid
me adieu.

Can you fulfill just one last
wish of my shattered heart?
Before I leave this world, will
we meet once before we part?
If God grants me the courage
to see you one last time,
I wouldn't want this life to
carry on without you—no
longer mine.

Never give your heart to
someone already broken,
For once they heal, their
wounds cut you open.

This world may see you as
egoistic or arrogant,
but they don't know the falls
you've endured.

Stay true to who you are,
until you reach where you
want to be.

Outshine yourself like the
warrior you are.
Take your time. Hustle.
But don't stop.

I won't say "move on" from
everything,
but I will say, move forward—
step by step.
Be the one who starts the
queue,
not the one who waits in it.
Be the reason the queue exists.

When love feels like a distant dream, And its warmth no longer seems meant for you, Do not waste your tomorrows craving its embrace. Instead, rise. Become the one who shapes the world, A force unstoppable—be it divine or damned.

Remember this: There is no more tomorrow

You think they'll feel your presence, But, my dear friend, people change—and sometimes for the worse. You are good, and that's why the world feels kind to you. No one can tell the depths of someone's heart just by their face; If they could, they'd be a god, not a mere human. Listen to yourself, and live for yourself. Life is short—make it vast with your purpose. Don't live for someone else's company; Learn to find completeness within your own.

What secret pulled you so far from me,
What mystery do you guard so silently?
What lies behind that hesitant smile,
That keeps you close yet a thousand miles?

Set aside this silence, and lay bare what you hide,
You warned me I'd burn to hear another's name
Then strike the match, let me feel the flames.

See my condition, life itself has
begun to weep,
How does this soul still survive
after their parting?
Death stands quietly behind,
whispering,
'This is why I had to arrive.'"

Hold patience close so love
doesn't feel absurd,
Let the divine embody love,
but never let love become
divine.

"A thousand times I lost them,
even before they walked away,
They would come to meet, but
love was never in their heart."

I don't know how to claim you
as mine,
Nor how to make you truly
align.
You say you belong to me,
Yet standing by me doesn't
come with ease.

If you knew how, you'd never
doubt,
Even in silence, you'd sort it
out.
You'd show me where your
heart resides,
Convince me I'm yours, with
no place to hide.

Even if I stayed quiet, you'd
call my name,
Through your words, you'd
ignite the flame.
If I were upset, you'd pull me
close,
With warmth that only your
embrace knows.

All night, they lay their head
on my shoulder, asking again
and again, 'Why can't I see that
star?' Now that they're gone, I
spend my nights counting stars
alone.

I am my own worst enemy,
What harm could you ever do
to me?
I erased your name from my
very soul, Now only God will
settle this toll.

No regrets linger in my heart,
Whether questions remain or
answers depart.
An innocent stood punished
for a crime unknown, While
the judge now loves someone
of his own.

For you, it's just a
heartbreaking verse;
For me, it's a complaint
whispered to someone who'll
never hear.

I tried to pen the ache you
bring,
But every word feels a hollow
thing.

A love that blossoms, yet
leaves a scar,
A memory that heals, but
never too far.

What could I ask of these
broken stars,
When you must be wishing,
too,
For the strength to forget me,
As they shatter and fade from
view.

I read a thousand books of
love to forget you,
Yet every page I turned
brought love anew.

A thousand times I fell for the
words they spun,
Only to find you in everyone.

They looks at me and breaks
into tears,
Life can be so cruel—it takes
away those we hold dear.
Every time I tried, love left me
defeated,
My fate is such that wherever
love awaits, it's there it fades,
depleted.

A painted smile, a trembling heart,
A love once whole, is now torn
apart.
Fragile threads of a bond once tight,
Now scattered ashes in the fading
light.

Dreams that sparkled, now heavy
with cost,
A future once promised, forever
lost.
Fear like whispers, shadows that
cling,
Echoes of heartbreak, a cruel sting.

A wound so deep, it dares not heal,
Love's sweet fire turned cold and
surreal.
Unanswered questions, profound
silence,
a ghostly ache where love was found.

Will your gaze hold the warmth I
knew
Or the shards of pain you left in
view?
A labyrinth of sorrow, no light
remains,
Just a haunted heart and its endless
chains.

They left as if they'd never
return,
now they're back as if they'll
never leave.
In this cycle of coming and
going,
there's a heart they keep
breaking, again and again.

How do I make them
understand?
They may come and go as they
please,
but this heart can never be
theirs again.

Why does this night return
again and again?
There's no peace even in its
stillness, plain.
It comes each time to remind
me anew,
That now, I no longer have
you.

Once, it held calm, a gentle
embrace,
Now, only your memory takes
its place.
How can I say we're not
together anymore?
All that's left for me is this
night, nothing more.

They flow through every vein of mine, and my eyes ache just to see them. If they met me happily, this life would feel a little less like life.

You said, “New day, new me,”
So why aren’t you living by
it? Why are you still stuck in
memories? It’s easy to say,
“Forget everything and move
on,” But only the one who
suffers knows the effort it takes
to break free.

Still, I assure you, Once you let
go of those bonds, You’ll rise
and shine like a star.

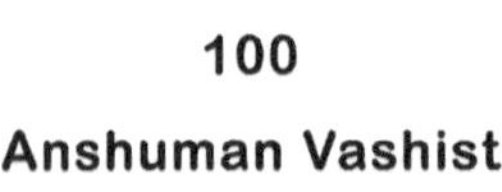

What did you earn by being
good every time?
Nothing—just a tag, a
villainous crime.
They cast you as bad, no
matter your cause,
A pawn in their games, bound
by their laws.

So, be the bad they cannot
break,
The storm they fear, the choice
they forsake.
Love or respect will come your
way,
For the unconquered always
hold sway.

They belonged to another sky,
another moon,
Yet I gazed at them, lost in my
own tune.

Called them mine, in their
light I'd stay,
Letting life pass softly, dream
by day.

Whenever clouds of their
choosing would veil,
I'd wait in the shadows, let
hope prevail.

But they drifted away with the
clouds, set free,
While I wove dreams of a
moon meant for me.

A war of words,
yet again, the silence returns—
unchanged, unbroken.

No answer to the letter I bared
my soul to,
no whisper of solace, no trace
of you.
Only this quiet messenger,
its silence heavier than a
thousand storms.

It speaks no name,
perhaps you've taught it fear
too well.
Or is it me who trembles—
at the weight of your
indifference?
Your hatred, so artfully
nurtured,
so fiercely alive,
tears through what's left of me.

A war of words,
but the victor is clear—
your absence, your eternal
refusal
to come back to me.

You saw how much pain I was in after you left, Yet you kept blaming me for everything. I lost everything that was mine, And still, I kept giving it all away for you. I gave up everything I had, And when I lost you, I realized That you were the one I needed to lose, For sometimes, losing everything is the only way to gain it all.

Why do my prayers fall silent
and fade?
Why aren't you mine, why this
endless shade?
Each day, I whisper your name
to the skies,
Does God not listen, or are
these empty cries?

My heart clings to a faint, cruel
lie,
That one day you'll be here,
that you'll come by.
But why does this hope refuse
to die,
When all I seek is you, and
only you, nearby?

I'd give the world just to call
you mine,
Yet somehow, we're strangers,
bound by time.

Go, tell them for me to forgive,
and not to return in memories.
All I ever did was love; that
was never a crime,
yet here I am, sentenced to die
each day by the weight of their
memory

If you come and hold me close,
I swear, the divine will feel so
close.
I'll abandon the world, its
rules, its ties,
In your love, I'll dissolve,
where my soul lies.

Let my love turn into worship
for them,
Let their presence become my
breath, my anthem.

So entwined, I can't live
without their trace,
Their habit, my soul's
permanent embrace.

If I call their name, may it bind
destiny tight,
And have them rush to me,
erasing every fight.

Let them be mine in every
possible way,
May my belonging to them
become their need one day.

They came to lift my will,
They came to bring back my
strength still.

A little late was their arrival,
For the Divine had come
before,
To witness my soul's revival.

If you ever find a moment
of peace with yourself, come
meet me one last time. But
if you must seek someone
else's counsel to decide, stay
with them, not mine. And
please, don't tether my name
to a love that now belongs to
another. I'm already drowning
in silence; don't bury me any
further.

I bled words, staining them
red, to win their heart,
But they came only to tear
mine apart.
This aching soul now weeps in
despair,
Begging for a touch, a moment
to repair.

Yet, they don't turn, don't
glance my way,
For whom I wandered, night
and day.
I loved with every vein, every
thread of my being,
Only to be left with wounds
unseeing.

No longer will love be mine to
choose,
If not them, then there's
nothing to lose.
And so, I pen my final plea,
Let death now be the one to set
me free.

You're no longer the landscape
I see,
Without you, there's no world
for me.

I gave up the moon, the stars,
the sun,
In a realm without you, there's
simply none.

I've fallen from the skies, time
after time,
From heavens where your light
no longer shines.
An endless void, a silent
despair,
For where you aren't, nothing
is there.

My story has reached its quiet
demise,
For I lost you—the only prize.
No more defeats can shatter
my core,
For losing you was the final
war.

Teach me a spell, O bearer of
love so divine,
To weave their name forever
into mine.
That they, consumed by
longing, cannot bear apart,
Bound to me by the threads of
their heart.

Let me enchant their breath to
seek my air,
Turn my silence into their
whispered prayer.
Teach me to bind our souls in
a sacred embrace,
Where love becomes fate,
timeless in its grace.

I have crossed the river of love,
drowning within,
Ruined myself, and all I could
begin.
Set hearts ablaze in every
town,
only to be consumed, love
pulling me down.

I whispered rumors that love
devours the soul,
Yet I embraced it—and paid its
toll.

I was the flower in her
bouquet,
That fell to the ground and was
left to decay.

If you stay away, it's the hate
you give,
Yet waiting for you is the love
I live."

They came, draped in the hues
of my shroud,
Hands adorned with henna,
another's name spelled out.
They watched me dying, a
smirk on their face,
Lost in the joy of someone
else's embrace.
Hurry, my friends, light my
pyre tonight,
I can't bear to see them braid
their hair in delight.

They embraced another and
built a world anew,
With that, my own world
crumbled out of view.

Joy passes by the front of my
house,
She knows where I live, yet
never allows.

Seeing my tears, she looks back
once more,
Only to leave, her words
cutting me sore.

"Let this lover die," she mocks
my pain,
Her voice like thunder, her
words like rain.

She says, "Life knows nothing
of love's lore,"
While death stands waiting to
smile at my final door.

All the pain, all the wounds,
every mistake—I'll take them
all,
But before your name, I'll still
write love, standing tall.

You break my heart and smile
with someone new,
Yet call yourself loyal, while I
paint your image true.

Go now, to the one who caught
your eye,
Who outshined me in your
shallow sky.

To the world, I'll pen a
message clear,
Stay away from love—it only
brings tears.

I stood there, tears in my eyes,
pleading for love,
but that heart of stone held
firm, saying only this:
"Even if you were gone, it
wouldn't matter;
there are countless who care
for me,
and one less won't change a
thing."

So I stayed, holding my broken
heart in silence,
knowing I was nothing more
than a shadow,
waiting for a warmth that
would never come,
for a love that had never truly
been mine.

No one asks me, this silence
you carry—where does it come
from?
Why do you sit so quiet, as if
some shadow haunts you?
Did someone break your
heart, is that why you seem so
withered?
Or has a whisper pierced your
soul, or have you given your
heart away?

You left as if you were never
really here,
I shared the pain of your
leaving with no one nearby.
I've endured the weight of the
world's endless sorrow,
But never stained your name,
not today, not tomorrow.
If leaving me brings you joy,
then so be it, stay free,
As for me—what do I have, but
the emptiness you left inside
me?

Maybe they came into my life
only to teach me
Those promises sound
beautiful in words, but they
were never meant to be kept.

If they ever knew how deeply
I loved them, they'd beg the
heavens to bring me back. But
even the gods would whisper,
"The dead can never
return."

There's a weight on my chest
every night, the kind that sinks
into your bones.
I feel myself breaking each
day, yet all I want, even as the
pieces fall away, is you.
I hold on, not because I can't
let go, but because I'm haunted
by the thought that no one else
could love you with this depth.

I can't trust anyone else to
make you feel what I would,
to give you the happiness I
ache to give.
One word slips and I become
the villain in your eyes—
maybe I am flawed, maybe I'm
not perfect.
But even in my fractured,
imperfect state, know this:
"what's left of me is still
infinite in its love for you."

It seems our story is fading to
dust,
You are my last love, my final
trust.

I turned my heart to ashes in
the dust,
Perhaps, while gathering roses
not meant for us.

Their love once glowed like a
fire divine,
And I, in that blaze, erased all
trace of mine.

Now that they've drifted far
from my side,
I see how, in love, my soul
died.

But it's not the farewell that
haunts my night—
It's that the one I called life
became my final rite.

Today, I pray that somehow, we find our way back to each other. But what if that prayer is answered? What if we're together again, only for the same story to unfold? You'll come back, break me all over, then leave me stranded in those empty nights, where I'm left holding a cigarette, staring into the dark, whispering another prayer for you.

And so the cycle begins again—you shedding me whenever you can, and me, pleading with the heavens for one more chance to love you, to let you break me once more. It's almost tragic, isn't it? That you find joy in watching me hurt, and I find mine in seeing you happy, even if it's from breaking me.

You're so in love, aren't you,
That you forget the one you
miss Is smiling with someone
else,
As if you were never a part of
their life.

And here you are, tangled in
dreams,
Wishing for the day they'll
come back,
To hold you tight and melt
into your embrace,
Hoping to ease the ache that
never fades.

Your smile is etched in my
memory;
when I see it, I see a part of
myself reflected back.
I wanted to make you happy,
always, and I'm sorry I couldn't
do it every time.
But in the end, you left because
of my flaws.
I thought love would mean
forgiveness,
but love has become just
another word, and once again,
ego wins.

You were the moon, the one
everyone adored,
and I was the forgotten star,
fading quietly in your glow.
You were the light of heaven,
the one they all wished upon,
and I was the fire of hell, a
distant myth, never truly
believed.

I'll die without you.
Then die, they said.
That's how their love was.
At first, when I'd say, "I'll die
without you,"
They'd whisper, "Don't say
such things."
But today, there's no
difference—
No trace of care.

After you, I keep searching for
someone like you,
In a city of betrayal, I yearn to
find someone true.

But even if I find another with
your face and your ways, what
would I do?
I'd still be the fool, breaking all
over again, Just to be called the
broken one once more.

I'm still standing on the
platform where you left me,
alone. I know you're not
coming back— you've moved
on.

Yet somehow, this endless
waiting soothes me, because
in this moment, I'm still with
you. I'm still here, lost in the
memory of you, holding on to
the faint image that lets me see
you once more.

You took my scolding as
reason enough to leave,
filled yourself with bitterness
and locked me out.
But if you had looked past the
rough edges,
if you had seen the love buried
beneath,
maybe I could have shown you
the tenderness you needed—
instead of watching you slip
away

They only ever asked for a
shoulder, a place to rest their
weary head. How could they
have known, though, that if
they had held me just once,
I would have fallen apart
entirely in their arms?

When my heart never belonged to you, And you never stayed by my side, Why should I shed tears for you? Why should I adorn my nights for you? If you're leaving, then go ahead, What's the use of crying for you? You were the one who wanted more, But I came alone, and now I leave alone too.

How do I even speak of this
pain I bear?
How do I survive this storm,
pretending I don't care?
When I pour my heart into
words so true,
I smile a little, only to break
down anew.

I won't belong to anyone else
anymore,
You'll never find me wandering
through the alleys of your
heart's door.

Since you left, I haven't truly smiled.
I still know how to laugh, but it's empty.

If I could see you, I'd light up again,
But not seeing you is the reason behind all my pain.

They said, “I’ll see you
tomorrow,”
but that tomorrow never came.
I tried to write my fate beside
them,
but they never even told me
their name.
They say, “You don’t love me.”
Then what is this ache I carry,
if not love?
Every night, I die a little more,
fearing the loss of someone I’ve
already lost.

I loved you deeply, gave you all
I had, but in the end, all I got
was emptiness.
I gave you my whole heart, yet
when you left, you only listed
my flaws. It's strange, isn't it?
The one you loved most
became the one who hurt
you most, pointing out every
mistake, ignoring all the ways I
changed for you.
In the end, you made me out
to be the villain, while the pain
you caused goes unseen.

My heart beats louder, echoing
despair,
I know someone else has
touched your soul,
Yet I am powerless, For you are
not mine anymore,
I've lost you forever,
A void that time cannot
console.

They say I'm easily hurt, but
is that true? The pain within
runs deeper than any wound
another could leave. We carry
so much heartache inside that
a single, fleeting kindness
feels like love. Yet, the truth is
bitter:

they're just passing through,
offering a moment's warmth,
not a lifetime's promise.

People believe they deserve love, imagining it as someone arriving with flowers in hand. But love is not a person; it's a quiet poem we hear alone, a song echoing when the world fades to silence.

Love lives within us, though we search outside, hoping to find in others what already hides in our souls. We chase reflections, pouring our hearts into strangers, yet love waits patiently within, unseen and untouched. Only when we discover that hidden love inside can we finally recognize the true lover waiting beyond.

If I were to write the love I
hold for you on paper, Even
that page would surrender,
Becoming a vessel for the
weight of my longing, A silent
slave to the depths of your
love.

You are beautiful—if only you
could see yourself through my
eyes.
You'd see the most beautiful
person I've ever known,
but it's my gaze that frames you
in this light.
Your eyes, though, look at
me the same way they look at
everyone else.

I've closed my eyes, but
the birds don't sing for me
anymore.
I watch the shooting stars, but
their magic is gone;
they don't stir a single feeling
now.
Maybe somewhere, someone
else is wishing for me, maybe
someone else could love me.
But even the world seems to
know— I'm no longer allowed
to miss you.

The moment I saw them, I
knew it was the beginning of
my end.
I always knew they wouldn't
stay, but still, I held on to each
day,
Hoping for just one more
moment with them.

Now that they're gone, it feels
like they were never really
here,
Only the pain of their leaving
stays,
A wound that never heals, and
a love that was never mine to
keep.

The pain I carry is mine alone,
heavy and unsharable.
Loving you was a chapter
I cherished, a part of me I
thought was whole.

But the wound you left
behind? That's the scar
I forged, trusting you
completely, blindly, with all I
had.

Why is my patience being
tested today,
Whose love is it that keeps you
at bay?

Who is this that makes your
feet refuse the ground,
Who is this that makes you
sway, unbound?

The way you comfort others
when their hearts shatter, as if
the ache of someone leaving is
nothing at all,

I can only hope that someday,
someone loves you with a
tenderness that fills every
corner of your soul—and then
walks away, leaving you to
understand what words could
never heal.

I sold my soul to the devil just
to save you, while you gave
yourself away to a love made of
illusions,
lost in the hollow glow of
borrowed affection

The day you left, I forgot the sun, And now the night is my only friend, Wrapping me in shadows, blurring my view, Comfort found in darkness since you've gone.

Yet I believe one day the light will break, And I will rise to meet the sun again, Shining bright with a smile reborn, Emerging from this endless pain.

If only you could stay in my
life,
let the world keep the rest—
none of it matters. I have loved
only you,
no one else, if only my love for
you could withstand time.

You once asked me to bring
you the moon,
but all I have left is a shattered
mirror, a reflection of love,
now broken.
And yet, through all the
fragments, I still wish you love.

I wonder how some move on
so fast— finding someone new
while we're still haunted by
their memories.
How do they build new
moments with someone else,
while we're left clinging to
the past, holding on to them
alone?
Why is it that those who love
the deepest are always the ones
left behind, betrayed by the
very soul they thought would
be theirs forever?

Look into these eyes, stained
red with sorrow's flame,
I'm burning alive—behold my
ruin, my shame.

What should I seek to find
some peace?
When they draw near,
whispering, "In your hands
lies the name of someone
else."

I stand in fields of dandelions,
Whispering wishes with every fragile sigh,
Hoping each one carries the dream,
That one day, you'll be mine.

Yet the wind steals them away,
And with every gust, I ache,
For I fear you're a wish too far—
A dream destined to break.

When you blossom, even gold
feels fragrant,
And I, I fade like a whisper of
wine.
Your tears fall, turning to
pearls of sorrow,
But mine—mine spill as water,
lost in time.

In your laughter, there's the
glow of the moon,
While my cries linger in a
dark, endless night.
You bloom like a flower, pure
and bright,
And I, like autumn leaves, drift
out of sight.

I won the world; I have
everything I ever dreamed
of…

Until they left.

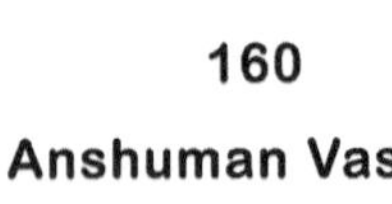

Oh, darling, trust me if you
will, but know that you
shouldn't.
I could lie a lifetime, so
seamlessly you'd never know
where truth and falsehood
met.
Not because I'm a liar— but
because I can't bear to see you
cry.

The story of my pain and
all I've endured I bury deep
within my heart, so all you
ever see on my face is a smile
woven from happiness,
while sorrow lies hidden, out
of sight.

"You still love them? Don't be a fool, move on," the world says.

But no, it's not love anymore—It's the wish to be near them just once more, To break my heart again in their presence, To rest my head on their shoulder and cry. I love only them, and I'll complain to them alone; If my tears are for them, then it's to them I'll turn, For only they can bear the sorrow they left behind.

My heart may be broken, but it
still beats, still belongs to me.
And if you weren't the one to
care for it, someone else will,
someone who understands its
worth.

Maybe you weren't meant for
it, but that doesn't make it any
less.
It's still whole in its own way,
and I will find someone who
deserves it.

I don't know if time will ever
be mine, but remember this—
I'll always be yours, even if
you'll never be mine.

People say that after they
drifted away from me, they
became even more beautiful,
As if nature itself is giving me
a sign, That I was the reason
behind all their sorrows,
their silent cries. I find myself
smiling through tears when I
see their picture, For the one
who has them now is truly
the blessed one, While I'm left
with nothing but the ache of
knowing I was the cause of
their grief, and someone else
now holds them when they
break.

I laugh, but my heart crumbles
with every smile,
They are more radiant now,
and I—lost in exile.

I carved out a chapter of life
Made you my beloved, my
very own light
Gave all that I could, without a
doubt
Yet all fate gave me was sorrow
throughout

Now that you're no longer by
my side
The only thought that haunts
my mind
Is this cruel truth, the weight
of grief—
How can a life end with just
one heart's brief?

Who is this adornment for,
dressed with such care?
And who brings forth that
smile you wear?
Who is it for whom you place
the bindi so fine,
And for whom does your
laughter brightly shine?

Someone take me, too, from
this world's call,
For my lifeless body waits by
her door, longing, after all.

They used to tell me that my
eyes were deep, that they could
see everything in them.
But when they left me alone at
the metro station, I don't know
what they saw in them then.

Maybe they forgot to look
for the pain, raw and red like
blood, pleading with them to
stay, just once more, to say
they loved me.
But they turned away, leaving
me there with nothing but the
hollow echo of their absence

If only you would read this
book of mine,

I swear on you, I'd stop writing
with this broken heart of mine.

Life's cruelty—unyielding,
that's you,
While I am cursed, beauty
shines through you.
The page where love's
confession was etched,
Even it proclaims, "Of all grace
and charm, none matches you.

- **All that I have left is Love**
BY Anshuman Vashist

Coming soon

Candles are meant to glow in celebrations, not to plead for justice.

- **The Super Villain**
BY Anshuman Vashist

Coming soon

www.ingramcontent.com/pod-product-compliance
Lightning Source LLC
LaVergne TN
LVHW091321150826
845673LV00006B/1721

* 9 7 9 8 8 9 6 3 2 8 3 9 1 *